B. P. Pratten

A Candid Enquiry Into the Present Ruined State of the French Monarchy

With remarks on the late despotick reduction of the interest of the national debt of France

B. P. Pratten

A Candid Enquiry Into the Present Ruined State of the French Monarchy
With remarks on the late despotick reduction of the interest of the national debt of France

ISBN/EAN: 9783337244033

Printed in Europe, USA, Canada, Australia, Japan

Cover: Foto ©ninafisch / pixelio.de

More available books at **www.hansebooks.com**

A CANDID ENQUIRY

INTO THE

PRESENT RUINED STATE

OF THE

FRENCH MONARCHY.

WITH

REMARKS

ON THE

Late defpotick Reduction of the Intereft of the National Debt of FRANCE.

" Pour que l'etat monarchique fe foûtienne, le luxe doit aller en croiffant, du laboreur à l'artifan, au negociant, aux nobles, aux magiftrats, aux grands feigneurs, aux traitans principaux, aux princes, fans quoi tout feroit perdu."

MONTESQUIEU.

LONDON:
Printed for J. ALMON, oppofite Burlington Houfe in Piccadilly.
M DCC LXX.

PREFACE

BY THE

EDITOR.

THE following letter was lately received from an English gentleman, who now resides, and has the greatest part of his life resided in France.

The person to whom it was wrote, presuming that all national power, and the happiness of individuals, are merely relative, and best known by comparison, he has, without any motive of private interest, given it to the publick, as he will do some other letters, which shortly he expects to receive on the same subject.

Every candid, impartial man will then judge, if there is any resemblance of the healthy florid, portrait, that was given the last winter of the French monarchy, by a timorous, desponding party in this country under the title of THE PRESENT STATE OF THE NATION.

That

Your Lordſhip is pleaſed to tell me, that my arguments firſt gave you conviction of the miſtake you had long been in, of entertaining too high notions of the preſent power and greatneſs of the French nation; and now deſire me to tranſmit to you in writing thoſe arguments, to convince ſome of your friends of birth and high rank in England, who are alſo prepoſſeſſed with the ſame too favourable, but ill-grounded opinion of the power of France.

But though a compliance with your Lordſhip's requeſt will afford no ſmall pleaſure to myſelf; and though I have reſided in this country the greateſt part of my life, and been in the occaſion to ſee the interior ſtate of the government of France, its operations and effects, at no great diſtance, yet I fear your Lordſhip has deſired of me a taſk, almoſt incompatible with thoſe few hours which my health will permit me to devote to ſo great an undertaking.

A declining ftate of health, now more than twenty years ago, was, as your Lordfhip may remember, my firft inducement to refide in this country; when from ficknefs, and a want of relifh for the pleafures and gaieties of the world, I refolved to divert my hours by more rational and beneficial amufements, and to gratify my curiofity by acquiring a clearer conception and knowledge of men and things: and in the purfuit of which nothing has afforded me greater pleafure and inftruction, than an enquiry into the caufes that have moft apparently contributed to the increafe and progrefs of national ftrength and power; and alfo to the decline of thofe ftates and kingdoms, which, for a time, had dazzled and awed the world with their fplendor and greatnefs, and then as rapidly funk again into that obfcurity and unimportance, from which originally they arofe.

In perufing hiftory, my Lord, I have found it to be little elfe than a recapitulation of the perpetually fluctuating state of national power and greatness; and that all states and kingdoms have arose, and again declined, from almost similar causes.

The glory and magnificence of the Greek and Roman empires, and of many other antient nations, which now lie buried in oblivion, we shall have no need to mention, as we shall find in some of our neighbouring states, wherein we are much more interested, sufficient to gratify our curiosity on this subject. The rapid decline of the Spanish and French monarchies, which have, in the two last centuries, acted the most distinguished parts in the affairs of Europe, are more immediate objects of our attention; and to the latter of these nations I shall, according to your Lordship's desire, confine my thoughts in this, and the *future* letters, I shall have the honour of transmitting to you.

After the dread of universal empire, caused by Charles the Fifth of Spain, and the profuse, extravagant conduct of his
son,

son, Philip the Second, the balance of power in Europe seemed to be so equally poized, as to remove any danger or fear of such universal conquests, as had in former ages rendered so many nations slaves to the power and vanity of one prince.

Louis the Fourteenth of France was the last sovereign in Europe, who alarmed the other princes in it with the danger of universal monarchy. Born at a time when all the neighbouring courts were sunk into a state of supineness and inactivity, favourable to the projects of a young ambitious monarch, he did not fail to take the advantage of it, and indulge the fondness he received from nature, of displaying his power, and acting the tyrant.

His ambition was indeed well supported by the abilities of his ministers, and the talents of his generals; but after making, for more than half a century, such efforts in war, and such profuse expences in peace, as none of his predecessors had ever attempted, he lost, in the decline of life,

that

that brilliant reputation of a great sovereign, with which, in the meridian of his reign, he had imposed upon and over-awed all Europe; and he descended to his grave, not with the character of a great or wise prince, but of the best *actor* of majesty that ever sat upon a throne.

The wise administrations of Richlieu and Mazarine, the decline of the power of Spain, and many other causes, conspired together to give him a power and superiority, with which he long insulted all his neighbours.

By nature turbulent, haughty, and insolent, he at last became as odious to all Europe, as he ought to have been detestable to his own people, for the wanton, profuse manner in which he trifled away their blood and their treasure.

But from the splendor of his court, the magnificence of his buildings, the encouragement of arts, and by all the exterior pomp and appearance of glory and superior greatness, the people, through their national vanity, were so intoxicated, and the delusion

delusion amongst them was so general, till the last years of his reign, that, even amongst the sober thinking men, very few of them, I believe, saw half the fatal consequences that would, in time, attend a reign of more than fifty years of the most absurd profusion, and ridiculous splendor, that the western nations had ever been witness to.

Louis the Fourteenth of France, like Philip the Second of Spain, left his successor a ruined nation. He left him, what was worse, his example and his principles of government, founded in ambition, in pride, in ostentation, and all the ridiculous shew and pageantry of state.

The regent of France, during the minority of the present king, by nature giddy, bold, and intrepid, ignorant of the distresses to which the nation, by the expensive war for the Spanish succession, was reduced, and hurried on by ambition to act the part of a sovereign, attempted, a few years after the tranquility of Europe was settled by the peace of Utrecht, to tear that crown from the brows of a prince of Bourbon, fettled on the throne of Spain, which Louis the Fourteenth had exhaufted the very vitals of his country to place there. The regent ftill did worfe. Uninformed of, and a ftranger to the wife principles of a modern ftatefman, he gave *public credit* many fatal wounds, which ftill are bleeding; and wantonly committed as many miftakes and frolicks with the finances of the nation, and the private fortunes of the people, as could well be preffed into fo fhort an adminiftration; for he expired, according to the anecdotes I have heard, in a rapture of pleafure, in the arms of his miftrefs, in the year one thoufand feven hundred and twenty-two.

The conduct of the regent, during the memorable tranfactions of the Miffifippi fcheme, will ever remain a monument of his folly, injuftice, and ambition. The wounds he then gave to the credit of France, were bitterly felt during the late war. They are ftill felt, and will continue

tinue to be fo, whilſt all the vices of the preſent form of government continue to ſubſiſt in the nation.

The preſent monarch of France, tho' untainted with the vain ambition of a hero and a conqueror, hath, by the reſtleſs temper and haughty diſpoſition of his miniſters, been involved, ſince his acceſſion, in two ſuch expenſive wars as hath entirely effuſed the ſmall ſhare of ſtrength and vigour, which the nation had recruited by the long peace that preceded them; and by the violent efforts he made in both, ſo ſuperior to, and inconſiſtent with, the debilitated ſtrength of his ſtate, that from a progreſs of the original vices of the government, the ruined condition of the landed intereſt, the heavy load of national debt, and the entire loſs of public credit, the French nation is now reduced to a more conſumptive and exhauſted ſtate than ſhe ever was before involved in: and as all the great pillars of the ſtate are now become corrupted and decayed, with an enormous weight of diſtreſſes preſſing upon

upon them, we shall, without the interposition of Providence, or some essential revolutions and changes in the present form and mode of her government, see, even in our own days, the French nation sink into the same state of nerveless indigence and poverty, which the Spanish monarchy hath long been buried in.

Insensible of their approaching fate, with a levity and folly constitutional to all ranks of that people, the present court of France have adopted the same splendid and ambitious notions of government, with which they had, during the happier and more vigorous times of the late reign, dazzled and imposed upon all their neighbours: but the deception, however, is now confined to themselves; and to such superficial statesmen and people of other countries, who take appearances for realities, and judge of the present power of France, from those short and transient periods of greatness, which shone forth with so much lustre during the meridian of the last reign:

The

The power by which they formerly, with so much insolence and haughtiness, took the lead in all the affairs of Europe, is now no more: the ambition only remains. To support appearances, they are now forced to strain every nerve of government; they maintain unnecessary, formidable armies, a splendid magnificent court, and in every department of the state, a most enormous and extravagant peace establishment, for the empty consolation of imposing upon their own people, and some of their rivals, with the appearances of a power, which (I hope to prove to your Lordship) is no more natural, or the effects of health and vigour, than the rouge, which is dawbed upon the face of a tawdry antiquated Duchess at Versailles is of youth and beauty; who may, in the justest sense of an allegory, be looked upon as an emblematic figure of the present state and political government of France; she, in her happier days, might have made conquests, and been an object of admiration; but to attempt it in the decline of life, when nature is exhausted, and health and beauty fled, by the arts only of the toilette, is such an imposition upon common sense, as raises no passions but contempt and ridicule.

The affairs of government in this country, my Lord, are all deception and delusion; and individuals, like the government, from their national vanity, and the example of their monarch, always live far above their estates and fortunes: but tho' all their magnificence is no more than splendid poverty, yet, so much do the French ministers, by various arts and expedients, keep up the appearances of a formidable power, that many men, who stood in high stations in the different courts of Europe, are, like some of your Lordship's friends in England, as much deceived and mistaken in their opinions of the present power of France, and in the same ridiculous degree as they have been partial to, and fond of, its language, its wines, its modes, its vices, and its follies.

So

So great indeed hath been the address and refined artifice of the ministers of France, in imposing upon mankind with the formidable appearances of their power, that, in confidence of the timidity of some former English ministers, we have had the mortification to see the *Pelhams*, more than once, sit trembling in their Chateau at *Lewes*, from a dread of an invasion; when, in fact, as well as true policy, they might not only have pulled the mask from the enemy's face, and discovered their smile of ridicule at our absurd fears, but have thrown the French into a real and much greater consternation, by playing the same game actually upon them.

In this observation, my Lord, I am confirmed by the events that happened in the last war: the great statesman and commoner, who so happily and gloriously conducted that war, well knew the infinite resources of our own opulent country, and all the false pretensions to power and greatness of its vain and feeble rivals. That able minister, sensible of the strength

of

of Great-Britain and the weakness of France, soon convinced our enemies he was not be imposed upon, like the *Pelhams*, with the false appearance of power: on the contrary, he, upon all occasions, treated them not only in the active part of the war, but in the farcical negociation they began for peace, in the year one thousand seven hundred and sixty-one, with a dignity consistent with his own, and the honour of the nation, in whose service he was engaged: so far from being intimidated with their idle menaces of an invasion, he smiled with contempt at their ridiculous affectation, and bravely invaded and insulted them upon their own coasts; which, after all their vain blusterings and seeming formidable preparations, they never had either courage or strength to put in execution upon ours. This invading them, upon their own coasts, my Lord, not only exposed their false pretensions to power, but also mortified their national vanity, and rendered them greater objects of ridicule in the eyes of their neighbours, than all

all the other losses and disgraces they sustained in the war.

These successes, my Lord, of the ministers of France, have always arose much more from subtilty and refined addrefs, in taking advantage of the favourable circumstances in the times, than from the weight and importance of their real strength and power: of the truth of which, the strange manner in which the present minister of France hath lately made the valuable acquisition of Corsica, whilst the nation is staggering under the burthens of the late war, is a striking proof: being sensible of the intestine troubles that now prevail, not only in England, but in every part of its extensive dominions, he well knows how to take the advantage of them. An acquisition so valuable as Corsica, and gained at so small an expence, hath given the minister (as his friends say) a supreme contempt for the councils of his rivals, and added greatly to the opinion of his own superior national strength and political addrefs.

An

An unjuftifiable invafion like this, upon an inoffenfive ftate, and free people, in a time of profound peace, would, under different circumftances of the times, have roufed the refentment of all Europe againft them, whatever cafuiftry and fophiftry they might have pleaded in defence of it. The whole world may remember, that their encroachments on the banks of the Ohio produced the firft fparks of fire which lighted up the flames of the late war, that fpread itfelf into the four quarters of the globe: fuch encroachment was furely of much lefs importance than the ifland of Corfica, from which, by its adjacent fituation, the French can now conftantly draw, at a very cheap rate, any quantity of the moft excellent fhip-timber they may want, for the fupply of the royal navy at Toulon; and which, before this acquifition, they had no other means of procuring, than what they could get, at an enormous expence, and a tedious delay of many months, from the groves of Norway.

An

An acquisition so valuable as Corsica, and obtained at so little expence, might flatter the vanity of a nation less susceptible of it than the French: but unhappily for the repose of Europe, the chief minister of France is so intoxicated with ambition, and conceptions of the superior power of his own country, and so ignorant of the real strength of his rivals, that he hath a knowledge yet to acquire, which of all others, is the most important and interesting for a wise minister to know.

What I mean, my Lord, is so happily explained by a noble author *, who wrote in this country, and whose letters I read with more pleasure, as I read them on the spot where they were written; his observations are so judicious, so agreeable to truth, and so applicable to the present state of the English and French nations, that I will make no apology for quoting them.

"The precise point of time, says this noble author, at which the scales of power be-

* Lord Bolingbroke.

D tween

tween rival nations turn, like that of the folstice in either tropic, is imperceptible to common obfervation; and in one cafe, as in the other, fome progrefs muft be made in the new direction, before the change is perceiv'd. They who are in the finking fcale, for in the political balance of power, unlike to all others, the fcale that is empty, finks, and that which is full, rifes; they who are in the finking fcale, do not eafily come off from the habitual prejudices of fuperior wealth and power, or fkill and courage; nor from the confidence thefe prejudices infpire. They who are in the rifing fcale, do not immediately feel their ftrength, nor affume that confidence in it, which fuccefsful experience afterwards gives them: they who are moft concerned to watch the variations of this balance, misjudge often in the fame manner, and from the fame prejudices. They continue to dread a power no longer able to hurt them, as the other continues to have no apprehenfions of a power that daily grows more formidable. Spain verified

this

this obfervation a little more than a century ago, when proud and poor, and enterprizing and feeble, fhe thought herfelf a match for France." And France, at the prefent time, my Lord, again confirms the obfervation; for exhaufted as fhe is, by the fame caufes which reduced Spain, fhe does not perceive her fcale of power funk, but ftill entertains the fame ambition and pride which formerly prevailed in the councils of Madrid.

The quarrels between modern nations, my Lord, are decided principally by a full and proper exertion of the finances of the contending parties; and the events of thofe numerous wars that have happened in Europe, fince the difcovery of the new world, are fufficient to convince every rational man, that thofe nations, which have the greateft refources in their commerce and wealth, will generally come off triumphant and victorious.

The brave inhabitants of Great Britain, are, my Lord, the only people in the world, who have ever united the knowledge and activity of war, with the laborious employments of agriculture and trade; and from thefe advantages alone, tho' they were but a handful of people compared to the number of their confederate enemies, fupported in the laft with the moft aftonifhing vigour and fuccefs, the moft active and extenfive war that ever yet happened amongft the powers of Europe. The fame of our arms, like that of our commerce, was carried into the four quarters of the world, and the Englifh banners were triumphantly flying even in the Manilla Iflands, the moft diftant part of the globe. From the effects of our commerce and our wealth, we not only alone ftood fingle in the quarrel againft the united force of France and Spain, but nobly fupported too the crowns of Pruffia and Portugal, which tottered on the heads of thofe princes, before they received our fupport and protection.

The national credit of England, my Lord, which is fo effential a caufe of its power and greatnefs, is a difcovery entirely

tirely new in the history of human affairs, and to consider it with all its amazing advantages, is the noblest monument of political wisdom, that ever yet was framed by mortal invention: it is not the abundance of the precious metals alone which constitute the riches of a State, as we may see by the present beggarly ruined situation of Spain and Portugal: those metals are no more than a representing *mark*, given in exchange for the wants and necessities of men: England, without a fatal possession of the mines of gold and silver, hath discovered a *mark* which represents them as effectually; and was it not for fear of appearing too warm in my admiration of this amazing discovery, I would say, that the shirt of the meanest peasant, when worn to rags, may, by the art of manufacture, be fabricated into Bank-bills and government securities, of more intrinsic value than the revenues of Potosi and Peru; for they, and the more precious stones that are dug out of the bowels

els of the earth, receive their value only from the opinions and estimation of men.

This credit of the French nation hath, on the contrary, my Lord, received so many fatal blows, by the wanton folly of the different ministers both in the last and present reign, that it is now no longer a resource of government; and from the want of this important succour, they received, in their last struggle with Great Britain, every distress and disgrace that could possibly attend the most unsuccessful war; she not only saw her commerce and marine entirely destroyed, but after those seeming vigorous efforts in the beginning of the war, which an absolute and a military government is, from the nature of its constitution, so well adapted to make, the vitals of the State were so soon exhausted, that so early in the war as the year one thousand seven hundred and fifty nine, she was reduced to the fatal necessity of shutting up her sinking fund, appropriated for the payments of the interest of her national debt, and to apply its produce

produce towards the expences of the war; and which, in spite of all the plausible excuses made by her ministers, was at best but a partial bankruptcy with her creditors, and did not fail to produce that effect; for, after that violence done to good faith and public credit, she was compelled to give the most exorbitant interest for money to all from whom it could be obtained; even for those sums that were borrowed upon the edicts, regiftered in the parliament of Paris, which then became the debts of the State. I have now before me proof, was it necessary, that she paid for it from ten to twelve per cent. interest; and for those great sums lent by the corporation-towns, collective bodies of men, and the rich individuals, upon the king's personal security (a superficial mode of credit, which you in England are unacquainted with) the interest was still more exorbitant; and for want of ready money to go to market for the supply of her armies and navy, the contractors for both did not make less than from

sixty

sixty to seventy per cent. on their bargains: reduced as she was for want of money, she at last had no better resource than that contemptible expedient of melting down the plate of her people; and which, from the most favourable accounts of the different mints, did not produce more than between six and seven hundred thousand pounds sterling: but the taxes were so exorbitant, so numerous, and so sensibly felt, that the load was at last become insupportable: for at the time of the peace, the people were even staggering under the burthen of a third vingtieme, and a double capitation: circumstances of such distress and oppression as had never before happened since the existence of that monarchy.

In a former part of this letter, I just hinted to your Lordship, that the power and internal strength of nations were best known by their wars and quarrels with their neighbours; for then only they make a full exertion of their wealth and their finances: but whatever, my Lord, may be be the fucceffes of a war, the advantages at laft reaped from it, fatal experience hath fhewn, are feldom adequate to the expences of the blood and treafure of it: for war is a game that may be played fo many different ways; it admits of fo many various expedients, even with the neighbouring powers, not engaged in it; the paffions, the caprices, the follies, and even the different fentiments of wife men are fo effentially concerned in, and mixed with its operations, that at the conclufion, it is, of all things, the moft difficult to tear, even from a ruined and exhaufted enemy, an equivalent for the lofs of blood and treafure expended in it.

Our own nation, my Lord, hath acquired as much honour in its quarrels, as any other kingdom can boaft of; but the conquefts, that bring glory to its armies, may alfo bring diftreffes upon the ftate, to which they belong. The country where I now refide, my Lord, hath gained more by fome of its wars, within the laft century, than any other nation in Europe:

E the

the trifling expence, both in blood and treafure, of the late acquifition of Corfica, is known to every one; the conqueſt of Alſace of Franche Comté, and of the Spaniſh low countries, by the late fovereign of France, and the important acquifition of the principality of Lorraine by the prefent, were, in no degree, as to expence of conqueſt, equal to their value and real eſtimation; which, upon the moſt moderate computation, as to refources of revenue, number of people, and advantage of fituation, may be higher eſteemed, than all the acquifitions we gained by thofe two obſtinate and expenfive wars, for the Spaniſh fucceſſion at the opening of the prefent century, and that which terminated at Fontainebleau in the year one thoufand feven hundred and fixty three, though our arms, in both of them, were attended with the moſt brilliant and amazing fuccefs. But as we had made, in thofe two wars, as many great and important conqueſts, as could well be crouded into the number of years they laſted, I leave it

to

to the historians of future ages to enquire, why we did not draw from them greater advantages.

Insensibly, my Lord, I have wandered from the subject I first set out upon and proposed to entertain you with: but this digression, however long, will serve at least to convince your Lordship's friends, how greatly the state of the French nation appeared, by its conduct and resources, to be enfeebled and worn out by the late war, in comparison to the strength and vigour of the firm and robust government of Great Britain; whose luxuries and vices have not yet enervated and unstrung the great principles of its constitution.

But should these general outlines of the circumstances of the two nations, during the violent efforts of the late war, have no weight in the opinion of your Lordship's friends, to shew that France is an exhausted state, I shall, to convince them of it, now enter into a more circumstantial detail.

Yet

Yet to avoid, as much as poffible, prolixity, and tiring your Lordfhip's patience, I fhall prefs my matter clofe; and only give you thofe remarks in a general way, which your own good fenfe and knowledge of the fubject will enable you to draw every neceffary influence from. In this, my Lord, I fhall follow the advice of the immortal author of the Spirit of Laws, who judicioufly fays, " il s'agir de faire penfer; plutot que de faire lire," an advice, I have often been forry, that hath not been followed by the writers of his own nation, who, to my great mortification and lofs of time, have frequently reverfed the wife maxim of the great author juft alluded to.

The landed intereft being the great fountain and fource from which the power and opulence of the ftate, and the fupport and happinefs of individuals, do, in every wife government, fpring, I will, firft, my Lord, begin with the prefent ftate of the agriculture of France.

The kingdom of France, my Lord, including the countries annexed to it, during the late and the prefent reigns, contains, according to the moſt exact calculations, about one hundred and forty millions of Engliſh acres, and the number of its inhabitants, according to the famous Marſhal Vauban, are about twenty millions.

The compact fituation of France; its extent of country; the advantages of its climate; the richnefs of its foil, in producing, in fome of the provinces, filk, corn, wine and oil, and almoſt every article to gratify either the neceſſaries or luxuries of life; the beauty and grandeur of all the great roads leading from the moſt diſtant parts of the kingdom to the capital; the advantage of fo many rivers and canals, formed by nature and art, and particularly that of Languedoc, which is in length an hundred and fixty Engliſh miles, and lays open a communication between the Mediterranean fea, and the great weſtern ocean; the ingenuity, induſtry, and fubordi-
nation

nation of its people; its vicinity to Spain, and other nations, who, by inland carriage, take off their rich manufactures and other products; the superior excellence of their sugar islands, which bring them an amazing profit, as they do not consume a third part of their product themselves; the great encouragement given to the arts and sciences, and even to every trifling profession, that tends to polish and refine the exterior appearances of life; the art of inviting and encouraging the subjects of the neighbouring nations into their armies and manufactures, by which their industry and number of inhabitants are increased; and, above all, the infatuated fondness which all the Courts, as well as people of fortune in Europe, have adopted for the rich manufactures of France, and all the other products of tinsel shew and magnificence, for which the French nation have been so long famous; and what hath still turned more to the advantage of France, few foreigners of rank and fortune are content with enjoying the modes and manufactures

nufactures of it in their own countries, but do, in some part of their lives, pay a visit to this land of luxury and politeness, to taste its pleasures and learn its language and manners; nor is the enormous sum of money, spent in France on these occasions, the only advantage the French reap from such visits; for foreigners acquire there such a fondness for the modes, manners and manufactures of that country, that they continue attached to them to the detriment of those in their own nations, for the remaining part of their lives; all these advantages, my Lord, are certainly great; and they have been extolled and sounded high by the gay and giddy part of the nobility in our own as well as in other neighbouring states; but by none so much as the French nation, and the French ministers themselves; who, intoxicated with these superficial advantages, have neglected those in which their real power and prosperity were more deeply concerned.

Though the extent of country in France, and the number of its people are three times

times as great as in England, yet, I am well convinced, that the annual produce of the landed interest in England is vastly superior to that of France*; for with all the advantages of soil and climate, which they enjoy, their land is not half cultivated; for the follies and vices in their government conspire together to prevent the progress of the landed interest.

It is from a want of wise maxims and laws, relative to agriculture, that the present landed interest of France is now sunk into such a low and consumptive state: Of what use have their numerous armies in time of peace been, but to destroy that very power they are so ambitious of supporting? And though in the last, and in the present reign, they have added to their monarchy some great acquisitions, yet from the vicious and impolitic rules and

---

* The annual product of the land in France, is calculated by Vauban Mirabeau, and their ablest writers, at fifty millions sterling; that of England alone, since our late amazing improvements, is valued at between seventy and eighty millions.

methods

methods of their government, which they have established in those acquisitions, they have added very little real power to the state.

Unhappily for their neighbours, and the repose of Europe, the great object of the ambition of the French ministers hath always been to extend their territories, and neglect the improvement of the fertile soil, they had already in possession; and which, in extent, is sufficient to support with food, and every necessary and luxury of life, more than double the number of their inhabitants. Had they extended their territories ten times as far, and, from a want of judgment and wise laws, neglected to procure a proper number of farmers and husbandmen to cultivate them, whatever reputation it might have given to their armies, which alone they are ambitious of maintaining, it would have added little or nothing to their internal power.

All the arts, subtleties, and superior address, even of the ministers of France, on which the French have almoft totally depended for the aggrand:zement of their ftate, cannot, without an induftrious application to agriculture, procure food for their foldiers and people: and the government that neglects this moft important of all advantages, muft, whatever fplendid appearances they may, for a fhort time, put on and deceive their rivals with, be in poffeffion of a power very precarious and unfubftantial.

The efforts made by the great *Sully*, to cultivate and improve the landed intereft of France, was attended with fuch fuccefs in his own time, and was in fo flourifhing a ftate, relative to the then neglected condition of our own, and other countries, that when Colbert, a little more than a century ago, was called into adminiftration, the French fupplied with corn, not only our own, but all the other markets in Europe.

But Colbert, not content with this great and permanent advantage, determined, in compliance with the vanity and oftentation

tion of his ambitious fovereign, to build the future power and glory of France on an encouragement of the fine arts, an eftablifhment of fumptuous and coftly manufactures, and all thofe other objects of tafte and refinement, that are moft fubfervient to pomp and luxury ; and this, with a defign to lay all the courts of Europe under a contribution to his own.

The nature, principles, and benefits of commerce, being not at that time fo well underftood as at prefent, his plan appeared to fuperficial capacities, both plaufible and wife : but to fupport this expenfive new-adopted fyftem, and bring it to perfection, he, for the fake of encouraging thefe manufactures in their infantftate, was reduced to the neceffity of loading, by heavy and arbitrary taxes, the landed intereft.

The errors of great men are, in affairs of government, much more fatal in their confequences than thofe of an inferior capacity ; thus Colbert, to encourage thofe manufactures, upon which he hoped to build his future fame with posterity, had recourse to another operation, the most wild and extravagant that ever entered the head of a great statesman; well knowing, that the price of manufactures will ever depend upon the price of labour, and the price of labour upon the plenty or scarceness of bread and other food, he erroneously concluded, that by entirely prohibiting the exportation of corn, it could not fail, in the event, to render it more abundant and cheaper in the market; and by this means, that the manufacturer would be enabled to afford his industry at so moderate a price, as not to be equalled by their rivals in trade; but by this false conclusion, he brought on a decline of the agriculture of France, and by his successors in power following the same mistaken conduct, the landed interest of France hath been thrown into such a languishing state, as the abilities of the greatest ministers may never recover it out of.

Whilst

Whilft the progrefs that agriculture hath made in England, fince that time, and particularly fince the law for allowing a bounty on the exportation of corn, is amazing; and is entirely owing to the miftaken conduct of our rivals on this important object.

Since the ruin of the landed intereft in France, their minifters, when alarmed with a great fcarcity of corn, and danger of a famine, have had no other refource, than, at the expence of government, to fupply their magazines and public granaries from England, or fome other country, rich with the products of agriculture, and retailing it again at a moderate price to their ftarving people.

Our own nation, my Lord, happier in its opinions and operations on this moft important of all objects of government, hath, without public granaries, or any fuch trifling and fuperficial refources, difcovered, upon the furface of the earth, mines of more real wealth and value, than the precious metals that lie concealed in its bowels; which, besides feeding our own inhabitants, and diffusing plenty and opulence through all ranks of our people, does not fail to keep the proud lords and proprietors of those mines, as well as our vain and haughty rivals, the French, in a state of dependance upon us for their very support and existence.

England, my Lord, is the only state, either antient or modern, that hath made wise laws and regulations for the increase and improvement of the landed interest: and experience hath shewn, that scarcity and famine have much more frequently happened in those countries, where the greatest precautions have been taken to guard against them, than in our own, where we even allow a bounty to our merchants to encourage them to export that very article of life, which is so necessary for supporting the existence of our own people; a measure the most bold and intrepid that ever yet entered into the mind of a legislator, and which, at first, so staggered and surpassed the limited conceptions

tions of our rivals, that nothing but the amazing advantages, which have refulted from it to this kingdom, could have convinced them of its wifdom and utility.

Since the paffing of that wife law for allowing a bounty upon the exportation of corn, and the farmers, from the happy effects of it, have been enabled to underfell other nations in foreign markets, when our own have been overftocked, our landed intereft, and our national ftrength have increafed to a degree unknown to any other country but our own.

This exportation of corn hath been fo far from raifing the price of it at home, as fome people at firft erroneoufly imagined, that it hath both augmented its quantity, and lowered its price, as may be feen by confulting the regifter of the price of corn for the laft eighty years.

Happily for England, the effects of this bounty upon the exportation of corn, hath produced an increafe of it, even more than equal to the increafe of our national riches; and had it not produced that effect,

fect, the consequences of those riches, by increasing the prices of the necessaries of life, would have been more severely felt, and more loudly complained of, even than they have been; for the price of the necessaries of life, as well as of the luxuries of it, will always be in proportion, and relative to the quantity of money, whether paper or coin, that circulates in a nation. When the productions of nature are, in any country, great and abundant, and money in that country is little and scarce, much of the former may be bought for a small quantity of the latter; but when the money of a kingdom shall be plenty, either from a discovery of mines, or a large quantity of paper-money, which answers the same end as gold, shall suddenly be brought into circulation, as is the case in England, it is obvious to common sense, without the aid of political arithmetick, that a larger quantity of money must be employed to purchase the wants and necessaries of life, than when there was but a little cash in the king-

kingdom; and this increafed ftate of the national riches in England, is, undoubtedly, the principal caufe of the complaints of the common people, that every thing is grown fo exceffively dear.

The great trade which England hath long been in poffeffion of, from the exportation of its corn, and the great balance it hath received in confequence thereof, was the reafon that the fcarcity of the harvefts, which hath, of late years, been general in all the countries of Europe, was more fenfibly felt by the people of England, than by thofe nations, who are more accuftomed to fuch fcarcity, and have not had the advantage of a foreign exportation.

However, during the laft four years in France, the fcarcity of corn hath been a very ferious and alarming circumftance; for their crops having fallen fhorter than ufual, and all other nations being unable to fupply their wants, it did not fail to produce great anxiety and folicitude amongft the higher ranks of people, and too often a ſtate of riot and confuſion a-mongſt the lower.

The harveſt of the preſent year hath been very favourable, and from the reports of thoſe who have been employed by government to enquire into its productions, it is believed, there will be nearly ſufficient for their annual conſumption; for even France, my Lord, with all its advantages of ſoil and climate, and the full enjoyment of the trade of their coſtly and ſumptuous manufactures, hath, amongſt other nations, been laid under contribution to us, and in the midſt of all her ſeeming grandeur, hath, within the laſt fourſcore years, paid us near two hundred millions of livres of their money, which is a ballance of more than a hundred thouſand pounds ſterling a year. But this ſum, your Lordſhip's friends will, with ſome appearance of truth, ſay, is but trifling, when compared to the enormous ſums we have paid the French for their wines, their baubles, and their rich manufactures of every kind.

But the ſpecific ſum, acquired by the balance

balance of trade, is not, as your Lordship well knows, of so much consequence to the power of a state, as the number of people, and the number of ships, it hath employed, and given a support to; a few bales of the rich manufactures of Lyons, might have produced to the French a more considerable sum than this balance of our corn trade; but he would be but superficially acquainted with the true advantages of trade, who should conclude, it was a matter of indifference to a government, or to a people, how the balance was produced.

The advantages arising from the landed interest, as I have before said, are more solid and permanent, and in which not only our support, but our very existence is immediately concerned; whilst those, arising from manufactures, especially such as are subservient to luxury and ostentation, depend only upon the folly, the caprice, and the mode of the times; and they too are easily imitated by other nations; and however infatuated the nobility of our own country have been to the

splen-

splendid manufactures of France, the present taste and elegance of those now produced by your own rich fabricks of silks and velvets in England, are, I am convinced, by some patterns I have lately seen here, equal in beauty, and superior in quality to those of Lyons: and as other nations have also imitated them with good success, the superb city of Lyons, in which the famous Colbert had placed his future fame, hath, within my own memory, like the state of France itself, been sinking and declining so very fast, that now it manufactures little more than is consumed by the French themselves.

The proud city of Lyons, which hath long made so great a figure in trade and commerce, will, it is more than probable, soon experience the same fate, as the once opulent city of Sevile hath met with; which, though now sunk from the vices of the Spanish government, into a state of poverty, had, but a century and half ago, according to Don Jeronomo d'Uztariz, a writer of great reputation, within its walls, not less than eight thousand looms,

looms, conſtantly employed in her coſtly rich manufactures, with which ſhe ſupplied all the nations in Europe; and however formal and pedantic the preſent Spaniſh dreſs may appear in the eyes of refined moderns, Spain was at that time, in its dreſs, as well as its language and manners, the model for all the courts of Europe.

France, about the beginning of the laſt reign, ſucceeded Spain in theſe great advantages; and with them hath long carried her head aloft, and over-awed her neighbours; but as national modes are always taken from thoſe ſtates who take the lead in power, even the haughty court of France hath, ſince the laſt peace, laid down its antient pride and inſolence to adopt our language, our modes, and our dreſs, though not our laws, and wiſe maxims of government.

Whatever, my Lord, may have been the fluctuating ſtate of power in other countries, yet as England is the only nation, either ancient or modern, that hath fixed the baſis of her power upon the landed intereſt,

it

it may be truly said, she hath laid the foundation of her power upon a rock. And from the natural advantages of its insular situation, its happy form of government, its wise body of laws, a marine that in power far surpasses any the world ever saw, and an extensive and useful commerce, not confined only to those objects that depend upon the changeable follies and caprices of mankind, but to those also of food and warm cloathing, which are the universal want of all nations; tho' none but our own, from the quantity of corn and wool it produces, is able to supply them. From all these advantages, that we enjoy independent of and superior to every other nation, I shall not, I hope, incur the censure of any national partiality from your Lordship's friends, in declaring, that the power and opulence of the English nation are fixed upon a rock that will be as durable as time itself; and not subject to decay and perish like that of the Spanish and French nations; which were rapid in their rise and decline of greatness; and who, after having shone with

splen-

splendor and figured it awhile in the eyes of their neighbours, are now almost dwindled, " like the baseless fabric of a vision," into nothing.

At least, my Lord, we are convinced from the experience of the late war, that the foundation of our government is not to be shook by the confederated power of the feeble, though in appearance formidable, *pacte de famille:* and if ever we should fall into those ruins, which so many other nations have experienced, it must alone be produced by our own internal diffentions, our own wanton folly and madness.

The power and strength of all political societies depending entirely upon the laws and maxims of their governments, it cannot be wondered at, that France should have long been in a declining state; for her ministers have attempted to raise a magnificent structure without the materials of the earth entering into the composition of it: the sandy foundation upon which it is built, hath been long evident from the dangers of famine to which their people,

people, during the laſt century, have been ſo often expoſed.

Since the time that Colbert's favourite ſyſtem was adopted, of raiſing the national power by the precarious riches ariſing from the trade and commerce of manufactures only, their landed intereſt has been in a declining ſtate; and ſo infatuated was that great man to this commercial idea, that he would, with pleaſure, have ſeen all the labouring people in the country changed into artiſts and manufacturers ‖. And, indeed, he laid upon thoſe employed in the uſeful branches of agriculture ſuch great and oppreſſive taxes, as ſoon compelled them to forſake a profeſſion where they found it impoſſible, with the utmoſt efforts of induſtry, to procure a comfortable ſubſiſtence. Since that time more than two-fifths of the country-people of

‖ A certain Engliſh ambaſſador at the court of France, upon viſiting the famous manufacture of the Goblin's in Paris, was aſked with a vanity peculiar to that nation, how he approved of the elegance of their tapeſtry? To which he ſhrewdly replied, that Colbert, to conſole the people for want of bread, had at leaſt feaſted their eyes and their imaginations.

France

France have, by the moſt moderate calculation, reſided in the towns and cities: and this removal was perfectly agreeable to his wiſhes, not doubting, but the aſſembling great numbers of people together, would be of the greateſt national advantage, by giving them imaginary wants, which, without the ſhew and diſplay of vanity and ambition, they never would have had, by living unconnected in the ſobriety of a country life.

Though the riches of a ſtate may depend upon the induſtry of its people, yet they do not leſs depend upon wiſe laws in dividing the inhabitants into ſuch claſſes as are moſt proper and neceſſary for ſupplying the wants and neceſſities of mankind: and though a manufacturer in France may procure, by his induſtry, a more eaſy and comfortable living for himſelf, than a huſbandman employed in the toils of agriculture, yet the advantages ariſing from the latter, are infinitely more ſerviceable to the ſtate; as he, by his induſtry, creates a value that did not before subsist, and which is immediately relative to the support and existence of society: and every nation, who, like [the French, do not take care that their people may have a sufficiency of bread, and the first necessaries of life, must always be in possession of a power that is weak and precarious. The proportion of the number of people in France, employed in their different manufactures, is, when compared to those employed in agriculture, and the numberless branches of industry relative to it, vastly unequal: but the arbitrary and oppressive taxes which the labouring people are exposed to, drive them from the cultivation of the land, to seek for a more easy and comfortable subsistence in those professions, which, so far from being useful and advantageous to the state, are a great expence and burthen to it.

The army, the church, the great body of the law, and its numerous dependants, the collecting the taxes, and the swarms of people employed in the king's farms of
the

the public revenues, drain the villages of almoſt one third part of their uſeful labourers.

Refined as the French nation is in all the ſuperficial and exterior appearances and accompliſhments of life, one cannot, without aſtoniſhment, look into all the abſurdities and abuſes of their form of government, and the unprofitable manner of employing their people.

But of all their abſurdities, their method of impoſing taxes for the ſervice of the ſtate, is the moſt abſurd; for thoſe, whom they ought in good policy to tax, are exempted from taxation; and thoſe, who ſhould be exempted from taxes, are moſt grievouſly burthened with them.

In France, the nobility, the gentry, the clergy, all the great proprietors of land, and every perſon holding any ſort of employment under the ſtate, are exempted from the taille, or the land-tax, whilſt the inferior ranks of freeholders, and all the lower and ſubordinate claſſes of people, who, in common policy, ought as much

much as possible to be spared, are oppressed by it in the most inhuman manner: even the day-labourers, who are not possessed of land, have a tax upon their industry, in proportion to what it is supposed they may, by the sweat of their brows, acquire: and it is a fundamental principle of the French government, that the lower classes of people must be kept poor, to secure their obedience to the state, and to force them to hard labour. This doctrine, however right and easy it may appear to ministers pampered with all the delicacies of life, is certainly carried to extremes, very inconsistent with true policy and the real interest of the state: for the peasants and labouring people, are, from their constant fatigues, and want of proper food to recruit their strength, exhausted and worn out, even before the age of fifty: the robust and full-fed people, who labour at the plough in England, would hear with astonishment, that the same classes of people in France, never taste any other reward for the sweat

of

of their brows, and the curse of their existence, than a scanty support of bread, and water, and roots.

Under oppressions like these, it is not much to be wondered at, that the peasants fly from the toils of agriculture to seek refuge in the towns, the army, or any other employments where a better support may be more easily obtained: and was there not such a strong and strict barrier, placed at all the frontier towns of the whole kingdom, to prevent any labouring people from passing, without giving security for their return, it is more than probable, that the French nation would be very soon deserted by all that class of people; who, properly employed and treated, constitute the real riches of a state.

In despotic governments, the absolute power of the sovereign is delegated to all persons who are employed under the crown: and in France each province hath its tyrant, under the title of Intendant: to him an absolute power is given to govern its interior state, and to levy the taille,

the

the capitation, and ſuch other taxes as are not included in the general farms. And in each pariſh, this deſpotic intendant hath a deſpotic ſub-delegate, who, being acquainted with the fortunes and properties of his fellow pariſhioners, hath an abſolute power to draw from them, not a certain and fixed rate in proportion to their ſeveral properties, but ſuch ſum as he ſhall be pleaſed to think they can, that year, ſpare for the ſervice of the king; and the people think themſelves happy, when this ſum does not exceed eight ſhillings in the pound of their annual revenue, whether ſuch revenue ariſes from property, or the effects of induſtry; and if the following year, the people ſhould, by plentiful harveſts, the efforts of induſtry, or any other favourable circumſtances, improve their properties, ſtill the king's collector hath a diſcretionary power to draw from them ſuch a proportionate ſum of that encreaſe as he ſhall judge neceſſary for the ſervice of the king.

This

This arbitrary and oppreffive tax, which the French call the taile, had its origin in the feudal laws, and was a tax paid by the vaffals in lieu of military fervice; and as the idea of vaffalage and contempt is, by the fuperior claffes of people, ftill annexed to thofe who pay it; and as every employment under the king, however fubordinate it may be, gives an exemption from it, it is the object of every man's endeavours to get clear of what is fo oppreffive and contemptible.

The many fatal effects of this abfurd tax, fo flattering to thofe born in the rank of gentlemen, and fo degrading and oppreffive to thofe who pay it, have been long perceived by fome of their wifeft minifters; and more than once it hath been propofed to abolifh it, and inftead thereof to inftitute a land-tax of fo many fhillings in the pound, upon an eftimate of the value of all the lands in the kingdom; and this tax not to be difcretionary and in the power of the intendant to encreafe or diminifh, as his caprice or intereft might direct,

rect, but to be at a determined and fixed rate in proportion to the value of the lands.

But many objections more plaufible, than juft, have always been made to this equitable propofal: the advocates for the continuance of the taille, under its prefent oppreffive mode, affert, that from its long exiftence, it is become familiar and habitual; and it is fo interwoven with all the great principles of their government, that it cannot be now feparated without new modeling the whole ftate; that the privileges of the nobility, gentry, and thofe who enjoy an exemption from it, are, by length of time, fo confirmed, that they would efteem it as the greateft injury imaginable, to be taxed under the fame mode and form with the lower claffes of people; that it would break down and deftroy thofe diftinctions of rank, which have exifted ever fince the beginning of the monarchy, and have added fo much to the fplendor of the crown; and that in abfolute governments, the lower claffes of people muft be kept in a ftate of indigence to force them to hard labour, and compel them to a due ftate of fubjection to their governors and fuperiors.

Many other fpecious reafons, equally weak and ridiculous, as thofe before affigned, have been given in fupport and maintenance of this abfurd and oppreffive tax; but the true reafon of its continuance, and why it will probably ever be continued, is the powerful influence, that the nobility, the clergy, and the great proprietors of land have in the affairs of government, and the particular advantages they enjoy by an exemption from it.

The nation who hath adopted principles of government like thefe, fo repugnant to its landed intereft, and who hold it as a maxim of policy to keep the lower ranks of their people in a ftate of poverty, can never be a formidable rival, either in time of peace or war, to a nation like England: and the French, notwithftanding all their encouragements given to the cultivation of the arts and fciences, and all the refinements of the pleafures and luxuries

luxuries of life, are yet in a ſtate of Gothick ignorance of that eſſential knowledge, which moſt contributes to the power and riches of a ſtate, and to the proſperity and happineſs of a people *.

The miniſters of France have been ſo far from improving and cultivating their landed intereſt, as common policy would direct, that they have always thought the power of a ſtate depended alone upon the ſtrength of formidable armies: and their vanity to take the lead in all the important affairs of Europe, and their propenſity to quarrel with their neighbours, have been the cauſe of their keeping up and ſupporting more numerous armies, than have been either conſiſtent with their revenues, or real neceſſity: the old peace-eſtabliſhment for the army of France was, till within theſe few years paſt, never leſs than

* The immortal Monteſquieu has wiſely obſerved; pour l'etat monarchique ſe ſoûtienne, le luxe doit aller en croiſſant, du laboreur à l'artiſan, au negociant, aux nobles, aux magiſtrats, aux grand ſeigneurs, aux traitans principaux, aux princes, ſans quoi tout ſeroit perdu.

two

two hundred thousand men: but the enormous expence of it being of late more sensibly felt by the government than ever, it was, after the late peace, to the surprise and chagrin of all the old advocates for military power and grandeur, reduced so low as an hundred and twenty thousand men; and which is a number surely more than doubly sufficient to garrison all their frontier towns in time of peace.

The great degree of honour that is annexed to the military profession in France, and the desire of avoiding every imputation of a want of personal courage, are the motives which engage the nobility and gentlemen of all ranks to serve the King in the army, almost at their own expence; for the pecuniary appointments in the service are very unequal to the great expences of it: for all the officers, who are of opulent fortunes, go forth to war with so much pomp and splendor, and such an extravagant number of servants and horses, that they expose themselves, with great justice, to the ridicule of their enemies, who cannot see the use or benefit of so much
splen-

splendor and magnificence in a profession where they are very little wanted, and ought to be but little encouraged.

It hath been thought, by superficial people, a profound policy in the French government, to animate their troops to serve from a motive of honour, rather than a pecuniary reward; but this is not the only instance where the measures of the French government are plausible and advantageous in appearance, but yet produce very different and contrary effects: for troops must be properly supported, or they will never do their duty; and the daily pay of a French soldier, being only five sols, or two pence half-penny English, it is not sufficient to supply the wants of nature; and therefore the rest must be, some way or other, got from government, or from the industry of the labouring people: for he who supposes that a French army of an hundred thousand men are maintained at a less expence to their government, than the same number of English troops, considers the subject parally tially, and as only relative to their pay, and without knowing the privileges, indulgencies, and exemptions, which are granted to the military profeſſion in France, and which fall heavy upon the people.

Beſides, for want of annual cloathing, and a proper healthy food to ſupport the troops under the fatigues of war, the French hoſpitals ſoon become crowded with ſick and diſabled men, in a proportion of more than two to one, when the armies of both nations are equal in numbers; and few men but know, that a ſick ſoldier in the hoſpital is of double expence to government to one that is in health, and able to do his duty.

The enormous expence of the French military hoſpitals, during the late war, and of all their other contracts, both for the army and navy, when compared to our own, ſurpaſſes all belief; that ſome few of our own contractors accumulated great fortunes, is well known; but what even thoſe few men got, may be ſaid to be nothing at all, when compared to the
immenſe

immenſe fortunes, acquired by the French entrepreneurs; nor is it to be wondered at; for if men of high rank in the adminiſtration of affairs in France, will ſuffer their favourites and relations to require and accept of great conſiderations for obtaining lucrative bargains from the contractors of every ſpecies, it is not to be wondered at that ſuch contractors ſhould take every advantage of repaying themſelves by plundering the ſtate, when they can do ſo with great eaſe, and the utmoſt ſafety? For all theſe contracts being made under the authority of the ſovereign, no perſon whoever, dares to complain of their abuſe.

In compliance with the national vanity and natural foibles of the French, the nobility and gentry in France, do, it muſt be acknowledged, ruin their fortunes in the army with great chearfulneſs and alacrity; and in return for doing ſo, and the dangers they have undergone, every officer who hath ſerved twenty years without reproach, is intitled to the military order

order of St. Louis: and however trifling this bauble may appear in the eyes of the sober thinking people of other nations, the value of it is, by the arts of the ministers, kept up so high in France, that few gentlemen of fortune in that kingdom engage in the service with any other motive, than that of obtaining this badge of honour; and which, to animate their troops during the last war, was so profusely given away by the court, that now the number of that order exceeds nine thousand; for the officers of the navy, as well as those of the army, are equally entitled to it.

No sooner is this badge of honour obtained by officers, who are a little independent in their fortunes, than they retire from the service to enjoy their laurels in the circle of their friends and acquaintances: and this vanity, connected with many other follies of the military government in France, is the principal cause, that their officers are but little acquainted with the grounds and principles of the art of war, in comparison to their rivals; where men enter the army, as a profession for life, and propose, by acquiring a thorough knowledge of their employments, to advance their future fortunes; a motive, which, of all others would appear the most unworthy to an officer in France, who ruins his fortune in the service, and in doing so contributes to the ruin of the state, only from the ridiculous motives of vanity, which custom hath established in that kingdom.

The immense expence to government, in supporting such a numerous army in time of peace, is not the only bad effect it produces to the state; for the superior degree of honour and respect, which every military man in France is intitled to, intoxicates all ranks of people, and makes them desirous of embracing a military life; and which, not being an employment in France, either favourable to the morals, or the virtues of useful sober citizens, they contract thereby such habits of gallantry and dissipation, as are very inconsistent

sistent with the stations and characters of discreet country-gentlemen and sober farmers; in which capacities they would, by cultivating their lands and improving their paternal estates, be of infinitely more service to their country. Besides, all their common soldiers, being drawn from the great corps of husbandmen, are, from an absurd custom, not easily reconciled to common sense, inlisted to serve the king only for six years, which occasions a constant circulation of debauching * and ruining the morals and industry of the lower ranks of people; who, by living that time in indolence and laziness, contract such habits as render them afterwards very unfit for the labour and fatigues of agriculture.

It is but justice to own, that the French are more free from the effects of religious

* A French peasant, that has been a soldier, when again he returns to live in his own village, then becomes a bully, a bravo, and a bad member of society: and the French king looses more of this class of his subjects by the sword, in one week, for they too are men of honor, than are hung up at Tyburn in one year.

superstition, than those of any other Roman Catholick country in Europe; yet this does not proceed from a want of ecclesiastics to fill their minds with prejudices, but from their national levity: for though all the useless professions in France are abundantly stored with people, yet, the ecclesiastic profession, by far surpasses that of every other in number: for the younger sons of gentlemen embrace an ecclesiastic life, to enjoy in profusion and luxury the church-livings; and the lower classes of people enter into it from a motive of laziness, and as an exemption from the toils and fatigues of a laborious life.

According to the most moderate calculation, there are in France no less than five hundred thousand of its subjects, of both sexes, constantly devoted to a life of religion and laziness; who contribute nothing, either by their industry or population, to the benefit of society: the annual revenues of the church-lands, and those belonging to convents and religious societies, do, by a late estimate, amount to to eight millions sterling a year; and had not a law been made some years ago, to prevent ecclesiastics from either purchasing of more lands, or receiving from the weak and superstitious part of the people, legacies to the church, the priests and clergy would, by their pious frauds, have soon been in possession of three fourths of the lands and riches of the whole kingdom.

The church-lands, and the property in general of the clergy, being exempted from the greatest part of the taxes and burthens of the people, it is no wonder that such a collective body of men should be very opulent and rich : but the riches of the clergy in France, like those of the nation in general, are most partially and unequally divided. If the annual revenues of the church, which amount to eight millions sterling, were equally divided amongst five hundred thousand people, of which number the ecclesiastic community consists, it would bring to each the sum of sixteen pounds sterling a year, which would be sufficient, at least, to procure them all the wants and necessaries of life; but in the great body of the clergy, there are no less than an hundred and thirty one archbishops and bishops, who, together with those of other superior orders in the church, enjoy enormous revenues; whilst all in the lower and subordinate classes, live in a state of want and indigence, derogatory to the character of clergymen, and do, with difficulty, procure the common necessaries of life; whilst those of the higher orders are pampered with all the luxuries and delicacies of it, and exceed all other ranks of men in the kingdom in splendor, profusion, and extravagance.

It hath long been the object of the French government, to prevail upon their clergy to submit to the same modes and forms of taxation with the other subjects of the state; but, from the secret and powerful influence they have ever had at court, that great political object hath never yet been accomplished: the clergy,

from

from the great power and riches they poffefs, confider themfelves as *imperium in imperio*, and do, in their general affemblies, impofe upon their own body fuch taxes, and fuch fums, as they themfelves think requifite, out of their own revenues, to fupport the king's government: when this fum is thought by the minifters of ftate not equivalent to their poffeffions, they, to demonftrate their pretended zeal for the ftate, and avoid thofe contentions which might prove dangerous to their power, politically fupply the reft by what they call a *free gift* *.

The exeffive riches which are enjoyed by the higher ranks of the clergy, and the vaft number of people in the lower claffes

---

* It has often been propofed by the parliaments, to reform and diminifh the enormous power and riches of the clergy; but the hiftory of all nations, particularly thofe of the roman catholick religion, having furnifhed inftances of the danger of attacking even the abufes of the church, the court have rather fubmitted to them, than inflame the fanguinary enthufiaftick zeal of their Ravilliac's, their Clement's, or their Damien's.

that

that are supported in a state of indolence and idleness, are equally prejudicial to both population, and the progress of the landed interest; for the clergy, not being permitted to marry, are not so much interested to cultivate those immense quanties of lands they are proprietors of, as if those lands were in the possession of private citizens, who would, from paternal affection, exert their industry to provide for their posterity.

Of all the absurdities and follies in the French government, none have been the object of so much public clamour and discontent amongst the people, as the impolitic and oppressive mode of levying and collecting their taxes and public revenues: the customs, the excise, and many other branches of the public revenue are farmed out to a society of sixty men of the greatest monied interest in the kingdom. This contract is renewable every six years; and the present farmers pay to the king one hundred and thirty-two millions of livres, or six millions sterling a year, for the

pri-

privilege of plundering the ſtate: the only advantage to the government attending the preſent mode of collecting theſe taxes, is, that the farmers or financiers advance to the king the annual produce of the farms before they are collected: but the perpetual ſtate of indigence and want, which the government is in for money, is alone ſufficient, one ſhould think, for aboliſhing the continuance of a mode ſo pregnant with evils to the ſtate, and oppreſſions to the people.

The collecting of the cuſtoms and exciſe in England, and the other branches of its revenues, which correſpond to thoſe articles included in the farms of the French king, coſt the Engliſh government, according to a moderate computation, about ten or twelve per cent. upon the ſum collected: but it hath been demonſtrated, to the conviction of every unprejudiced man in France, that though the King receives from his farmers only ſix millions ſterling a year, yet, by the amazing abuſes and enormous profits of the farmers, the people

people are charged with, and pay more than double that sum*: befides a lofs to the ftate, in employing more than an hundred thoufand of its labouring people in the fubordinate ranks of cuftom-houfe officers and fpies; who, from the virulence of the excife laws, and from a want of fome judicious reftraint or limitation, fret and teize the ufeful but unhappy people, with-

---

* A kind of political phrenzy feized the people in Paris, in the year 1764, to enquire into the abufes of the public revenues; and many fenfible performances at that time were publifhed, very little favorable, either to the integrity or abilities of the minifters. Amongft others, was a work intitled, L'Anti-Financier, which demonftrates, that the branch of the revenue, called, Les Aides, or Excife upon Strong Liquors, not even 20 per cent. of what was raifed upon the people, came into the king's coffers: thefe enquiries were fo very painful to the minifters, that they chofe to thunder out an ordonance, to forbid, under pain of the king's difpleafure, any body, for the future, to comment upon thofe fubjects which alone were cognizable by the king and his minifters: it is certain, no abfurdity can equal the impolitick manner the French raife their revenues, but the profufe manner in which they fquander them away.

out

out mercy; and which the unfeeling farmers totally disregard.

In a government but desirous of shewing even the appearances of justice to its people, the great abuses and heavy oppressions, which are daily practised in this department, could not a moment subsist, if the *great officers* of the state were not *themselves* deeply interested with the farmers in the contract. It is well known, that no person had so great a share in these profits, as the favourite Sultana, the late Madame de Pompadour; whose immense riches were acquired by being concerned in every transaction of government where money was to be got: and for the better accommodation of her passion for money, the late comptroller-general of the finances was raised to that important trust by her favour and protection only; that she might have every possible opportunity of gratifying her insatiable desire of riches.

He, in return, proved to her an obedient servant and a faithful friend, by obsequiously conniving at her tools and dependants,

pendants, buying up clandeftinely the
outftanding debts of the ftate, when fallen in the market to fifty per cent. below
par, and then paying them at the treafury, when in her poffeffion, at their original value: by fuch lucrative tranfactions as thefe, fhe, at her death, had amaffed more riches than were in the poffeffion
of any other fubject in Europe *.

Since the prefent mode of farming out
the publick revenues was eftablifhed in
France, all the great monied men in the
nation have turned their thoughts from
trade and agriculture, the only fources of
wealth to a ftate, to employ their fortunes
in the money tranfactions of government;
and from the conftant diftreffes of the
king, the financiers, or monied men, enjoy alone the fmiles and favours of the

---

* This enormous fortune, thus acquired by rapine and extortion, fhe left to her brother the Marquis de Marigini; who, though born only in the rank of *Bourgeois*, was, by the influence of his fifter, decorated with the *Cordon Blues*, though exprefsly againft the rules of that order, which requires the proof of fix generations of nobility.

court

court, whilſt the landed intereſt is in ſo declining a ſituation, that the beſt eſtates are ſold with difficulty, at twenty years purchaſe; and by a policy, not to be reconciled to common ſenſe, the huſbandmen, the labouring people, and every profeſſion that contributes moſt to induſtry, population, and the real riches of a ſtate, are oppreſſed and looked upon with contempt; and ſuch things only encouraged, as are relative to ſhew, pomp and magnificence.

However neceſſary it may be, that the government and court of France ſhould be ſupported with ſplendor and magnificence, the effects of it, it is certain, have been ſo univerſally ſpread, as to intoxicate the whole nation with the thoughts of nothing elſe but pomp and pageantry: the evil of this profuſion and extravagance, is not ſolely confined to the king's houſhold, though it is there moſt ſcandalouſly great; for in that department alone, a ſum, more than equal to the amount of the land-tax of all England, when at three ſhillings

shillings in the pound, is squandered away; and it hath, more than once, been the subject of remonstrance from the parliament of Paris to their monarch, who have repeatedly declared, it was not the part of a tender parent, or an affectionate sovereign, to suffer such enormous and useless profusion in his houshold, whilst the poor industrious subjects of the interior part of his kingdom were reduced to the most deplorable state of misery, in contributing, by arbitrary oppressions, and the want of the very necessaries of life, to support that excessive splendor and extravagance *.

Though

---

* The first act of the present comptroller general, on entering the department of the finances, was, reforming the enormous abuses that prevailed in the king's houshold (la maison du roy) which includes, as in a private family, every branch of his domestick expence.

He found upon the list of the master of horse, no less than twelve hundred horses, charged to the king, at so moderate a price as five shillings sterling a day for the support of each; but only nine hundred of these horses were found to exist in reality. In the

Though it may be thought right and neceffary to fupport the crown in every monarchy with a becoming magnificence, proportioned to the riches of the country, yet this fondnefs for pomp and fhew hath been fo extravagantly purfued in France, that it is the only object of emulation, which prevails amongft all ranks of the nobility; infomuch, that even the prefent chief minifter, with a levity that

the mafter of the great wardrobe's accounts, was annually charged fix hundred coftly fuits of cloaths for the king's ufe, which was thought to be fully fufficient for a prince, rather modeft in his drefs. Indeed, the mafter of the wardrobe, had a very plaufible excufe to make for this feeming profufion, which was, that feveral dependants of the other minifters, were quartered upon his profits. Not to be prolix, the abufe of all the fmaller articles of expence, throughout the whole houfhold, were equally great, for no lefs than eight thoufand pair of gloves were annually charged for the four Mefdames of France, the king's daughters.

This reform and infringement upon the perquifites of the courtiers, did not fail to raife in the palace as great a confpiracy againft the new comptroller general of the finances, as if he had been the greateft enemy of the ftate.

would

would be more excusable in a petit maitre, than a great statesman, piques himself in saying, "that his equipages and liveries are not only more costly than the king's, but that his houshold also is so numerous, that the servants of his servants have servants to attend them *."

In a nation where such excessive luxury as this prevails in all the higher ranks of its people, all the labouring industrious poor are kept in the greatest state of oppression to support it; where commerce, agriculture, and every useful profession are held in contempt, and the distinction of rank and nobility is the prevailing passion; and where the degree of noblesse may be purchased with a mode-

* The liveries of the servants of the minister, are, perhaps, more costly than the senatorial robes of the English peers. Is it to be wondered at, that in a nation where sentiments like these prevail, the landed interest should be lying in ruins: the money which ought to cultivate it, circulates only in canals of luxury; and the villages are drained of its inhabitants, which ought to supply the nation with bread and food, to be employed in those offices subservient only to pomp and magnificence.

rate

rate fortune, it is no wonder that trade and agriculture should decrease, and the degree of the noblesse become numerous.

The government of France hath itself greatly encouraged the national vanity of the people in their fondness for the rank of noblesse, for in an absolute monarchy, such as France, and where the distribution of property and fortune is so very unequal, that the people are but one degree removed from all the absurdities of the feudal laws, vast numbers of the noblesse must have been unavoidably created; but the French government have not been content with such increase; for, besides the antient * hereditary peers of the kingdom, and all the subordinate ranks of counts, marquises, and the proprietors of lordships and manors, who have always been, by their birth, intitled to the privileges of noblesse; the government have created a great va-

* The hereditary peers of France, who have seats in that assembly, are only fifty two in number; but the subordinate classes of the noblesse, exceed, upon a moderate computation, more than sixty thousand families.

riety

riety of very unneceffary civil employments, to which they have annexed the privileges of nobleffe; and which have been fold, and made a fatal refource of revenue, in times when the ftate hath been in great diftrefs for money.

That I may as little as poffible fatigue your Lordfhip's patience with the nature of thefe *charges* or civil employments, which from their number are now become one of the greateft burthens of the ftate in France, as well as an abfurd refource of revenue, happily unknown in England, I will enter into fuch a detail only, as may convey to your Lordfhip an idea of the impolicy of their inftitution.

The *charge*, or rank, for example, of one of the king's fecretaries, and of whom there are more than three hundred, is an employment merely honorary, and hath neither duty nor attendance annexed to it: Thefe *charges* are generally purchafed by the defcendants of thofe, who, by their fucceffes in trade or other circumftances, have acquired fortunes; and who, in compliance

pliance with the national vanity, are desirous of enjoying, by the privileges of noblesse, an exemption from the taille, and from that degree of contempt and oppression, to which they would have been exposed by continuing in the class of *Roturier*, in which they were born.

The purchase of this *charge*, or rank of one of the king's secretaries, is about five thousand pounds sterling; and produces annually to the purchaser no more than three and a half per cent. for his money; but to this *charge* is annexed honour and respect, and it is, like a freehold, hereditary in his family: but however advantageous this mode of borrowing money may appear upon a superficial view, it would not be difficult to demonstrate, that, by the privileges and exemptions annexed to these *charges*, and all the collateral disadvantages attending them, it would have been wiser in the government, and cheaper, to have paid ten per cent. for the money.

M The

The unequal diſtribution of the lands, and of the riches in general of the French nation muſt, with ſo many other cauſes conſpiring together, keep their agriculture in a miſerable ſtate : the power of the antient republicks, and of every wiſe nation, hath always proceeded from and depended on wiſe and ſolid laws and maxims : none but French miniſters are ſo ignorant as not to know, that ten thouſand acres of land, divided equally amongſt an hundred different people, would not only be better cultivated, and afford ſo many families all the neceſſaries of life, but contribute more to the revenues of the ſtate, than if they were only in the poſſeſſion of one proprietor.

Notwithſtanding the ſplendor of the Court of France, the profuſe way of living amongſt their firſt nobility, and the magnificence which appears in many of the cities and towns, there cannot be a clearer and ſtronger proof of the *radical vices*, and *real poverty of the ſtate*, than thoſe ſwarms of beggars that are every where to be ſeen through-

throughout the kingdom: but the oppreſſions of the labouring people, employed in agriculture, are ſo great from the exceſſive taxes, that they cannot, with the moſt violent efforts of induſtry, procure by it a a tollerable ſupport; and begging at the gates of the convents and religious houſes, where they diſtribute in alms, what is ſuperfluous to their own wants, is a more beneficial and comfortable profeſſion, than exhauſting their ſtrength in cultivating the ground, the fruits of which are torn from them to pamper in luxury and extravagance the higher ranks of people.

Wiſe laws and wiſe maxims of government can alone contribute to the improvement and encreaſe of the landed intereſt in any country: wherever that important object is properly attended to, there reſults from it, food, cloathing, riches, revenues, commerce, navigation, and every thing that raiſes and creates the real power and grandeur of a nation, and the proſperity and happineſs of its people.

It is now more than a century, that the French nation have neglected and difregarded the ftate of their agriculture; and notwithftanding they have had, during that time, frequent famines, and always a fcarcity of both corn and wool, they have even flattered themfelves, that the advantages which they reaped in fupplying all the courts and countries in Europe with their rich manufactures, and other objects of luxury, were more than a balance and equivalent for all fuch wants and difadvantages.

Experience hath, however, at laft convinced them of their impolicy, and of the errors of their national prejudices. They beheld, with furprize, the prodigious efforts which England made, during the laft war, and faw, with aftonifhment, that fhe raifed the fupplies for the laft year with the fame eafe fhe had done thofe for the firft; whilft France had exhaufted its ftrength and its vitals, even in the firft three years of the war: this could not fail to convince the prefent chief minifter of that

that country, who, though not poffeffed of the talents of a great ftatefman, hath a quicknefs of conception few men are endowed with: he juftly concluded, that as France had for more than a century fupplied all the courts of Europe with velvets, lace, brocades, and all the moft coftly and expenfive articles of commerce, and yet was inferior to England in national riches, ftrength and power, that fuch fuperiority could alone proceed from the benefits arifing from the more cultivated ftate of her landed intereft.

The French, thus at laft convinced of the advantages of agriculture, have, within a few years paft, made every poffible effort to raife their landed intereft out of that declining condition, in which it hath fo long lain: and as the example of the fovereign hath, in France, more influence with the people than the moft pofitive laws, the king himfelf hath, of late, condefcended to work at the plough, as an amufement, in the inclofures at one of his country palaces, and alfo hath lately been

feveral

several times present with the first nobles of his court, at some new experiments relative to agriculture, with the hopes of reviving a profession that tended so greatly to the power of his kingdom, and the happiness of his people.

It is well known, when the sovereign of France and his court, have adopted either a virtue or a vice, or even a mode of pleasure, it extends itself by degrees to the last ranks of the people in the kingdom: but whether the present taste for the pleasures of farming, adopted by the king, will be attended with that effect, time only can determine. The country gentlemen, however, are so sensible of its advantages, and the want of improvements, that in more than thirty different provinces, they have formed themselves into societies to promote the advancement of agriculture; and the best books in the English language on practical farming, have been translated into French, and dispersed *gratis* by these societies to the farmers,

mers, as a guide in the future mode of cultivating their lands.

And should the French miniſtry ſucceed in raiſing their landed intereſt from its preſent low and languiſhing condition, to a ſtate like our own, then indeed, but not till then, the French nation would become a formidable rival to the power of England: but your Lordſhip's own experience will convince you, that all the operations of the French government, are more plauſible in their appearances than profitable in their conſequences. And whilſt ſo many radical vices continue to infect every department of their government, whilſt the clergy are in poſſeſſion of ſo great a ſhare of the landed property of the kingdom, which is exempted from the greateſt part of the taxes raiſed for the ſupport of the ſtate; and whilſt five hundred thouſand people are maintained by that profeſſion in indolence and idleneſs, and who contribute nothing towards induſtry or population; whilſt the pleaſures and luxuries of the court engage a conſtant

ſtant reſidence there of all the firſt nobility; and all the ſecond ranks of people lead a life of pleaſure and diſſipation in the towns; whilſt the huſbandmen, and all the induſtrious labouring people lie under ſo many oppreſſions from partial and arbitrary taxes, and the whole country feel the deepeſt and moſt abject diſtreſs and poverty; whilſt all ranks of people in trade are looked upon, and treated with diſreſpect and contempt, by thoſe who live in a ſtate of eaſe and dependance upon the government; whilſt ſo many *charges*, or civil employments, are to be purchaſed by thoſe who have acquired money in trade, and which give them the privileges of nobleſſe, and an exemption from taxes; whilſt the general ſtate of their commerce and agriculture hath not a tenth part of the money employed in their different branches, as thoſe great cauſes of the power of a ſtate require; whilſt the greateſt number of the people find it more honourable and lucrative to forſake the moſt uſeful employments,

ments, and to enter into the army, the law, the church, and the employments in the finances, all which produce no new encreafe of power to the ftate; whilft the excefs of luxury continues amongft the higher ranks of the people, and the labouring poor dare not marry for fear of increafing their burthens in life; and the people in general aim at nothing more than living fingle and independent by a life-annuity; whilft the intereft of money is kept up fo high, that it can be applied to more lucrative ufes than either in trade or cultivating the land; whilft thefe vices and follies, my Lord, continue to exift, and all of them are fo interwoven with the very principles of their government, as hardly to be feperated, there is no probability, that the French nation can ever be formidable to England by the progrefs of their landed intereft.

And now, my Lord, I fhould proceed to fpeak of the prefent ftate of the monied intereft of France, and of its national debt; but it being rather too large a field for one letter, and might be too tiresome for your Lordship's perusal, I shall reserve it for the subject of my next: yet, as your noble friends have very probably entertained too advantageous notions of the power of France in this respect, I shall so far enter into it, as to afford them some idea of it.

The discovery of the new world hath produced so great a revolution in the maxims of state, and the customs and manners of the courts of Europe, that their power and grandeur seem now to depend chiefly upon commerce and the acquisition of riches; yet, by a paradox to be reconciled only by the events that have happened, the kingdoms of Spain and Portugal, who have been the sole possessors of the mines of gold and silver, have been, by the fatal possession, reduced to a state of indigence and poverty, whilst the commercial nations, who have acquired these precious metals from their proprietors by way of traffick, have, according to the proportion they have gained of

them

them, increased in their strength and power.

The English and French nations being not only the two states in Europe, who have drawn the greatest advantages from the discovery of the mines in the new world, but rival powers also; and as the riches of a state are now deemed the strength of it, as the one will generally be in proportion to the other, it is of the utmost importance for the English nation to know the real quantity of the riches of its rival, France.

According to the best calculations of the quantity of gold and silver now circulating, or being in France, it amounts to between sixty and seventy millions sterling: this sum, though large, is not sufficient, from the impolicy of the government, and its unequal distribution to support all the luxuries of the nation, to cultivate an extent of land of 140 millions of acres, and to put in motion the industry and commerce of twenty millions of inhabitants; nor have the French one third

third of a capital employed in their agriculture, or their commerce, that thofe objects would require to put them on as good a footing as thofe of England: the induſtry and the progrefs of the power of a nation, depend principally on the riches of it, and of their being properly employed; and however paradoxical it may appear, it might not be difficult to prove, that was the French nation double in extent of land and number of people, without any increafe of gold and filver, it would then be doubly poor and indigent to what it is at prefent: for every acre of land, as well as the induſtry of every individual, requires a certain fum of money to put it in action, and as the profits ariſing from two hundred pound employed in agriculture or commerce, will be double to thofe arifing only from one hundred, fo the nation that abounds moſt in riches, and employs them on thofe objects, that produce other riches, that did not before exiſt, will have a power fuperior to another nation that lefs abounds in money.

ney. By taking the general mafs or fum total of the riches of a nation, and comparing it with the number of its inhabitants, we fhall eafily find, whether the nation hath riches fufficient to put the induſtry of its people in motion.

On a fuppofition therefore that the money circulating, or being in France, amounts to fixty millions fterling, and that this fum was equally divided amongſt twenty millions of people, then each individual would have no more than three pounds to put his induftry and ingenuity in motion: but this, or even a lefs fum would be fufficient for the purpofe, was France unconnected in every refpect with other nations, and did not fo conftantly contend with, and attempt to rival England both in peace and war; for it is then that our fuperiority and advantages become fo evident.

Though the fum total of the circulating cafh in England, is computed at no more than twenty millions fterling, yet, by the wifdom of its government, and its punctuality

tuality in preferving its publick credit; fhe hath eftablifhed fuch a refource of paper-riches, as, in every refpect, anfwers the fame end as the metals of gold and filver: thefe paper-riches, added to the fum of its circulating cafh, create a fum total conftantly in circulation of one hundred and fixty millions fterling; and which, being divided equally amongft fix millions of its people, gives to each individual, the fum of twenty-feven pounds to put his induftry and ingenuity in motion: and this is the principal caufe of the advantages and the great fuperiority we enjoy over France as a rival nation.

During the exiftence of the Miffifiippi fcheme in France, in the years 1718 and 1719, there were more than three hundred millions fterling of paper-money circulating in that kingdom; and which produced in France the fame effects for that fhort time, as our increafe of riches have produced in England: for there was, during that time, fuch an induftry and activity among the people, as was never known

known before in France; lands, that are now fold for twenty years, were then increafed to eighty and ninety years purchafe.

But the foundation of that fcheme, being neither built upon the principles of wifdom, nor conducted agreeable to juftice, its fall was as rapid as its rife had been: it was a magnificent ftructure, raifed upon a fandy foundation in two years, which would have required two centuries to have brought it by degrees to perfection. The great principles upon which it was attempted, were judicious, and it failed principally through the follies of thofe who were concerned in it, and the vices inherent in an abfolute government. The national credit of France, received upon that occafion fuch a fatal wound, as will ever prevent it from being again a refource of government: and as it will be impoffible for France ever to acquire a fum of gold and filver equal to our paper-money, fhe muft for ever remain

main in a state of inferiority, when compared to England.

Great as the inconveniences are, which France experiences from the want of a larger sum of riches in the nation, yet this want is greatly increased by the unequal distribution of the riches they are in possession of; for whilst some few persons are enormously rich, and spend their riches in the most profuse luxury, all those professions that are most useful to the state, have not a tenth part sufficient to carry on their different employments.

Nothing hath contributed more to exhaust the French nation of its finances, than the frequent and expensive wars in which they have, during the last century, been engaged; and though their armies carry the appearance of being maintained at a less expence than those of other nations, yet the great abuses which prevail in all their contracts, and in every commercial branch relative to supplying the army, make the expences of supporting it superior to that of any other country.

In

In France, it is the object of every man's wish to enjoy a penfion under the king; it is not the emolument only, that is the motive of this defire, for though a court penfioner is in England, rather a term of difrefpect, yet in France it is efteemed an honour fo great, that every man afpires to it, who is fond of fame: and the number of penfioners are now fo vaftly increafed amongft all ranks of the people, from the princes of the blood down to ingenious mechanics, as to become a great, and, in the prefent deranged fituation of their finances, a moft infupportable load upon the ftate.

Though it is both wife and juft in a monarch, to whom the riches of a ftate are trufted, to recompence fuch men of talents and abilities, as have by their ftudies and inventions promoted what is ufeful, and ferved and advanced the conveniencies or interefts of fociety, yet, it muft be confeffed, that the able and ingenious in France, who have moft deferved the recompence of the court, are thofe who enjoy the leaft part of its favours.

Out of more than a million sterling, which the king of France annually pays in pensions, the greatest part is swallowed up by the indigence of the great people, who surround the throne, and the favourites and dependants of that perpetual succession of ministers, who have trod upon each others heels since the death of cardinal De Fleury.

The king's pensions have, since that time, been so scandalously prostituted, that it hath not been for the services which men of talents and distinguished merit, have rendered to the state, that have entitled them to pensions from the king, but the favour and patronage of the different ministers to their own dependants and parasites: if a man has been able by his skill in cookery, to please the languid appetite of a decrepid worn-out minister, in inventing a particular sauce, or hath any ways contributed to revive his expiring passions, or in procuring him some personal pleasures, it hath never failed by the influence of his patron, of obtaining him a pension from the king.

This

This abuſe was ſo great, and its burthen upon the ſtate ſo ſenſibly felt, that when M. De Silhouette* (the only wiſe revenue-

* M. De Silhouette, who acquired his knowledge as a revenue officer, by a long reſidence in England, was rather a favourite of the parliament, and the people of Paris, than of the miniſters of the court: in the midſt of their diſtreſſes and want of money, in the year 1759, when the king could procure none but upon the moſt exorbitant intereſt; he propoſed to the court, to borrow twenty ſeven millions ſterling, at ſix per cent. with a premium, if the court would conſent to the *mode* of borrowing it by the parliament, who offered to be guarantee to the people, for the ſecurity of the money; but the court unwilling to give an importance to the parliament, which it was not entitled to, refuſed the offer, and had recourſe for money to more ruinous meaſures: in truth, by the original conſtitution of the French government, the parliament of Paris is extremely limited in its power: they can, it is true, remonſtrate, and even refuſe to enregiſter the king's edicts; but if the ſovereign preſents himſelf in parliament, and holds what they call *a lit de juſtice*, a prerogative which the monarchs of France are tender of exerting, then his will becomes the law, even without the conſent of parliament.

Great as their contentions have been of late, there was a time, even within theſe few years, that the

venue-officer, the French have long had) came to the administration of the finances in the year 1759, he found himself under a necessity to prevail upon his sovereign to issue an ordonance for all those who held pensions under the king, to deliver in a declaration, and specify expressly therein, the services they had done, to entitle them to them; and a proper court of justice of the revenue officers, was appointed to enquire into the validity of their services, and by what means such pensions were acquired.

This enquiry opened such a scene of fraud, artifice, and abuse, as would, to to any other nation but the French, have appeared most scandalous and unjust; yet so powerful was the influence of the patronage, court shewed a great disposition to the parliament, both of reconciliation and harmony: but it soon appeared, that the more concessions were made to a body of men, accustomed to submission and obedience, the higher they rose in their expectations and demands; and then aimed at almost the same power and dignity as the parliament of England; since that time, the court have received their remonstrances with a becoming form and ceremony, and paid them no attention.

tronage, which the favourites of the court had upon this occasion, that even in this enquiry, so just and equitable, and at a time when the nation was distressed for money, and then staggering under the burthens of the war, that able minister could procure for the state but very small advantages, where so many great abuses were demonstrated; and the pensions of those only were diminished, who had the best pretensions for their continuance, whilst those who had proper patronage amongst the courtiers, escaped without any reduction: in France, those who promote the most useful arts which are relative to the advancement of agriculture and commerce, on which alone the riches and power of a state depend, are neglected and unrewarded; whilst enormous sums of the public money, arising from the sweat of the brows of the industrious and laborious poor, are applied to support the luxuries and elegant dissipations of those who surround the throne, and are most profusely squandered away upon the idle, vicious, and extravagant.

Nothing contributes more towards diminishing the use and advantage of the gold and silver metals which the French acquire by the balance of their trade, than their own confumption or method of applying fuch riches. All the nations in Europe united together, have not fo great a number of artifts employed in the gold and filver trade or manufacture, as in France: as pomp and fhew is the prevailing and darling paffion of all ranks of people in this country, thofe of a middling ftate of life abound more in plate than thofe of a much fuperior rank in England, who are fatisfied to be ferved in china, or the fine earthen wares ; and thefe immenfe quantities of plate, which are fo exceffively abundant in all the families of the firft diftinction, as well as of all other ranks of people, are as ufelefs to the government, and of as little benefit to the nation, as if they ftill continued in the mines from whence they were extracted.

It is computed, that the gold and filver plate in France, including that belonging to churches, and the immenfe

quantities

quantities employed in family uses by the extravagant vanity of the people, in decorating all the utensils belonging to the common necessaries of life with them, does not amount to a less sum than between sixty and seventy millions sterling, which is equal to the sum total of their circulating cash; if this sum, or even one half of it, was employed in improving their agriculture or their commerce, it would be of infinite advantage to the state: But it is the foible of the French nation to vie with, and emulate each other in pomp and profusion.

That able financier, M. De Silhouette, was so sensible of the disadvantages attending the application of so vast a quantity of gold and silver to domestick uses, and for the sake only of pomp and luxury, that an invitation was made to the people, during his administration, to shew the r zeal for the state, by bringing all the superfluous part of their gold and silver utensils to the mint, to have it coined into circulating cash; one half of its value was to be paid in ready money, and the

the other half to be lent to the king at four per cent. But such was the fondness of the people for their gold and silver utensils, that, though the scheme was conducted under every advantage to excite the people's patriotism, by publishing the names of those who shewed their zeal for the government by bringing in their plate, yet it did not produce more than six hundred thousand pounds sterling.

The quantity of money in a nation may be guessed at by the interest which people pay for the use of it; for the interest of money is dependant upon the quantity of it in circulation: when money is very plenty, interest will be low; when it is scarce, interest will be high. It is of the highest advantage to a nation, when the people of it can borrow money at a low interest, for then they may borrow it and employ it, either in trade or agriculture, and get thereby sufficient to live upon, besides paying the interest: but such is the general want of money in France, that it is with more difficulty procured there at six per cent. interest, than in England at four.

Having

Having given your Lordship in the foregoing, only a brief and concise view of the riches of the French nation, I shall, as soon as my health and time will permit, send you a particular estimate of the present state of the monied interest in France, the circumstances of their national debt, and every thing that is immediately relative to their revenues, their finances, and their resources of government; for as the real strength and power of rival nations is best known by a comparison of their revenues and resources, your Lordship's friends will then be convinced, that the present state of the finances of France is in a more deranged and exhausted condition, than even the state of its landed interest; and yet, by the superior address and ambition of the minister, the French still keep up the appearances of a formidable power, but which can impose upon those only who are easily deluded, and take appearances for realities.

Celebrated as the French nation hath been in some periods of the last century, for ministers of superior address and abilities,

lities, none of them ever equalled their present chief: I shall therefore conclude this letter, by giving your Lordship a short description of the character and conduct of the present first minister.

He is a man of exceſsive ambition and intrepidity, and of a moſt refined addreſs; and though brought up in a life of pleaſure and diſsipation in the army, and was, at the time he came into power, unacquainted with the firſt rudiments of government, yet, by the favour of his sovereign, he was entruſted to conduct both the late war, and the late peace. Born of a family in Lorrain, more diſtinguiſhed for its antiquity, than its opulence; he, soon after he came into power, surpaſsed all the other nobles in splendour and profusion; and became in a little time so intoxicated with pomp and oſtentation, as brought upon him the envy and hatred of all ranks of his fellow-ſubjects. With a succeſs never equalled by the great Richlieu himself, he hath trampled under foot the power and jealousy of all the princes of the blood; the diſcontents of the army;

my; the complaints of the hydra-headed clergy; and the resentments of all the collective bodies of men in the whole kingdom. Equally succesful in extricating his country out of a most unfortunate war, as in framing a formidable confederacy of all the princes of the blood of Bourbon into one family-compact, and reconciling the jealousy and hatred that had long subsisted between the courts of Vienna and Versailles, he now enjoys in full possession, a power, with which he would, like Louis, the fourteenth, insult all Europe, but that he is conscious, the resources of his country are too much exhausted to support his boundless ambition in any expensive projects.

I have the honour to be,

My Lord,

Your Lordship's,

&c. &c.

POSTSCRIPT.

Chantelou, Feb. 6, 1770.

IT is now more than two months, since I first sat down to write your Lordship the above letter, but the frequent intervals of bad health, have, till now, prevented my finishing it.

I well remember, it was an observation your Lordship frequently made, during your residence on this side the water, that the happiness of every state, particularly of those states, where the sovereigns are absolute, intirely depends on the personal characters of those men who are principal actors in the affairs of government: it may be allowed me then to remark, that some of the most judicious men in this country, who lived in the time of the regency, and with whom I frequently converse, pretend to to find a ftrange refemblance in the characters of the prefent chief minifter, and the late regent of France.

The adminiftrations of both, it is certain, form very interefting periods in the hiftory of this country.

The prefent chief minifter of France, *they fay*, without the knowledge or the fagacity of a profound ftatefman, has ventured upon a career of fuch defpotick conduct, as the moft intrepid of their former arbitrary minifters, would have trembled at: fo great, they add, is his contempt for the wife maxims of policy, tranfmitted down by his predeceffors in power, that like the regent, he is alone guided by the influence of power, and by events and occurrences as they happen.

But this pretended refemblance, it muft in charity be fuppofed, is ftronger in their political, than in their private characters; for if credit may be given to a noble Lord of our own nation, who, during his exile in this country, was often, it is faid, the regent's companion in his nocturnal revels,

revels, he was not a pattern of the strictest virtue.

" The successor (says this noble Lord *) to Louis the fourteenth of France, not to the throne, but to the sovereign power, was a mere rake, with some wit, but no morals; nay, with so little regard to them, that he made them a subject of ridicule in discourse, and appeared in his whole conduct, more profligate, if that could be, than he was in principle."

The present chief minister of France, ****************** too strong in power to attend to the remonstrances of the parliaments, or the murmurs and complaints of the people, pursues those objects of administration, which caprice, folly, or the convenience of the present moment alone dictates.

It was thought by all the sober thinking men in the nation, a violent exertion of power, when in the month of December one thousand seven hundred and sixty four,

* Bolingbroke's idea of a patriot king.

four, the national creditors were defrauded of ten per cent. of the interest of that money, which under all the legal forms of the constitution, had been lent to the king to support the state in its wants, and distresses.

That tax of ten per cent. was laid under a plausible pretence of forming a caisse d'amortisement, to liquidated and pay off the debt of the state, but tho' it has not produced less than six hundred thousand pounds sterling a year, so far from being employed to the use of its institution, it has been profusely squandered away in acts of generosity, to support the brilliant dissipations of the needy dependants of the court; and the king, by an edict of the last month, has now, for eight years, appropriated it to pay his own personal debts. When that caisse d'amortisement was established, M. De L'Averdy, the late comptroller general of the finances, a member, and great favourite in the parliament of Paris, for the activity he had shewn in the destruction of the jesuits,

then

then had fo much influence with the court, as to procure a committee out of the body of the parliament to be the truftees, and adminiftrators of the new finking funds, independant of the minifters of the court; but fuch is the feduction and influence of the court of Verfailles, that the committee itfelf, foon became as obfequious courtiers as the minifter could wifh.

But the operation of the finances in the month of December, one thoufand feven hundred and fixty four, violent and arbitrary as it was, is now buried in oblivion, by the greater defpotifm of fome late *arrets* which have caufed a ftrange confternation amongft all the creditors of the ftate.

By the *arret* of the eighteenth day of the laft month, it deprives of any future advantages, the proprietors and fucceffors of all the tontines, exifting from the year 1709 to that of 1759 included, which proprietors are now limited to receive their annuities only, without any encreafe from the death of others.

By

By the arret of January the 20th, thofe debts which were borrowed by the king, under all the legal forms, at five per cent. intereft, are now, by an act of power, for the future, to be only paid at two and a half per cent. without offering to the national creditors, their original debt, if they were not fatisfied with a reduction of the intereft.

The laft arret, which this day appeared, dated January the 29th, is a tax upon the penfions paid by the king; thofe amounting to the fum of fix hundred livres, fhall pay a tax of two fhillings in the pound; thofe from fix to twelve hundred livres, half a crown; thofe from twelve to eighteen hundred, four fhillings; and thofe of two thoufand four hundred livres and upwards, fhall pay fix fhillings in the pound.

The arret, my Lord, of January the 20th, has thrown the whole nation into a confternation, not to be expreffed, and befides the injury done to private individuals, has laid the axe to the root of their future

future credit, for now, to ufe an expreffion of the judicious Montefquieu, " they have cut down the tree to gather the fruit."

Thefe arrets, cruel and defpotic as they are, is only a prelude to fome others, which are daily expected to appear, and which, from the diftreffes of the ftate, and the caprice of the minifters, may, perhaps, be as tyrannical as that deteftable edict, thundered out by the late regent in the year 1719, by which every private citizen in the ftate, was compelled, under *pain of death*, to bring into the king's treafury. whatever fums of money he was poffeffed of, that exceeded five hundred livres.

Already five edicts and arrets, concerning a reform, and regulations in their finances, have appeared, during the courfe of the laft month; and ten more relative to the fame fubject, are expected within a few months more; the next edict, it is prefumed, will be a tax upon coaches, livery-fervants, upon parks, and hunting forefts;

forests; which hitherto, with most of the other objects of luxury, have escaped any contribution to the expences of government; the particulars of the future edicts and arrets, and the effects they will produce, shall be the subject of a future letter; till then, my Lord, once more, adieu.

FINIS.

www.ingramcontent.com/pod-product-compliance
Lightning Source LLC
Chambersburg PA
CBHW020130170426
43199CB00010B/707